TOUGH DOGS

GERMAN SHEPHERD DOGS

Julie Fiedler

The Rosen Publishing Group's
PowerKids Press™
New York

For Kamil

Published in 2006 by The Rosen Publishing Group, Inc.
29 East 21st Street, New York, NY 10010

First Edition

Editor: Jennifer Way
Book Design: Elana Davidian

Photo Credits: Cover (left) © Gerard Lacz/Animals Animals; Cover (right) Gabriel Caplan; p. 4 © Ulrike Schanz/Animals Animals; pp. 7, 19 © Jorg & Petra Wegner/Animals Animals; p. 8 © A. M. Rosati/Art Resource, NY; p. 11 © Swim Ink 2, LLC/Corbis; p. 12 © Tom Nebbia/Corbis; p. 15 (top) © GK Hart/Vikki Hart/Getty Images; p. 15 (bottom) © Tim Davis/Getty Images; p. 16 © Farrell Grehan/Corbis; p. 20 © Owen Franken/Corbis.

Library of Congress Cataloging-in-Publication Data

Fiedler, Julie.
German shepherd dogs / Julie Fiedler.— 1st ed.
p. cm. — (Tough dogs)
Includes bibliographical references and index. ISBN 1-4042-3121-8 (lib. bdg.)
1. German shepherd dog—Juvenile literature. I. Title.

SF429.G37F55 2006
636.737'6—dc22
2005000603

Manufactured in the United States of America

Contents

German shepherd dogs are one of the most popular breeds today. They are valued for their intelligence and their ability to work at jobs including policing, guarding, guiding, and search and rescue. They are also popular pets.

Meet the German Shepherd Dog

The German shepherd dog is an intelligent **breed** of dog known for its faithfulness and bravery. German shepherd dogs are also known for their strength and their willingness to work. They can easily be trained to do many jobs, such as working with the police, with search and rescue teams, and in **pet therapy**. They are also used as herding dogs. Herding was the job for which German shepherd dogs were originally **bred**.

German shepherd dogs also participate in contests that measure abilities such as obedience. Some people are afraid of German shepherd dogs, but do not let their big size fool you. They can be wonderful family pets. They are protective of their owners and they make great guard dogs. Their intelligence, energy, and boldness make them an extremely valuable breed that does well in many different activities.

What a German Shepherd Dog Looks Like

German shepherd dogs are large dogs with strong bodies. Adult male German shepherd dogs are usually 24 to 26 inches (61–66 cm) tall at the shoulder and weigh 75 to 95 pounds (34–43 kg). Adult female German shepherd dogs are smaller, usually 22 to 24 inches (56–61 cm) tall at the shoulder and weigh 66 to 78 pounds (30–35 kg).

German shepherd dogs have a special double coat. The outer layer is longer and coarser. It helps protect the dogs against wet weather. The inner layer, or undercoat, is soft and thick. It lays close to the skin, which helps keep them warm. Their coats are usually black and tan. German shepherd dogs have long, bushy tails.

German shepherd dogs also have long, pointed ears. Their eyes are usually brown. Their **muzzles** are wedge-shaped. These active dogs look like wolves, which are distant relatives of dogs.

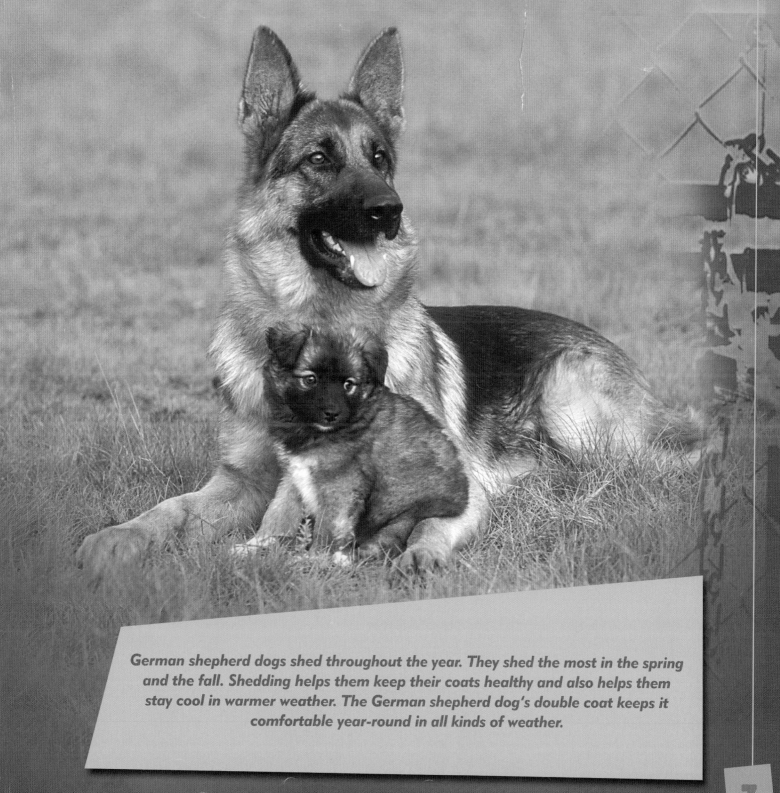

German shepherd dogs shed throughout the year. They shed the most in the spring and the fall. Shedding helps them keep their coats healthy and also helps them stay cool in warmer weather. The German shepherd dog's double coat keeps it comfortable year-round in all kinds of weather.

7

The large dogs that were ancestors of the German shepherd dog often helped people with such tasks as herding or hunting. This painting from the 1300s shows a hunting scene with large dogs helping the men.

Ancestors of the German Shepherd Dog

Scientists say that more than 15,000 years ago, there were wild dogs that were like wolves. These animals are believed to be the **ancestors** of today's dogs. As these wild animals were **domesticated**, they became an important part of people's lives. These dog ancestors helped guard people's homes and helped them hunt for food.

As time passed people wanted these dogs to help with different tasks, such as guarding livestock. Around 6,000 years ago, people began breeding these dogs especially for tasks such as herding or hunting. Throughout Europe, in countries such as Germany, Britain, and the Netherlands, people bred herding dogs to help them with their cattle. These herding dogs are the ancestors of today's German shepherd dogs. The German shepherd dog can be traced back to the late 1800s in Germany.

History of the German Shepherd Dog

In Germany in the late 1800s, a man named Max von Stephanitz was interested in sheep-herding dogs. Von Stephanitz wanted to breed different dogs together to create a great herding dog. In 1899, he bought a herding dog at a dog show and named him Horand. Horand was strong and energetic and von Stephanitz decided to breed Horand to create more dogs like him. Von Stephanitz called Horand and his offspring German shepherd dogs. Later that year von Stephanitz and a friend began the first club for German shepherd dogs. Horand was the first German shepherd dog to be listed in the club.

People soon learned about von Stephanitz's German shepherd dogs. The breed spread to other countries, and they quickly became popular in the United States. They are still one of the most popular breeds of dogs today.

By the early 1900s, people began to use German shepherd dogs for jobs other than herding. These new jobs included police work. This 1905 poster for a French play shows German shepherd dogs working with police.

German shepherd dogs are one of the breeds most popular with police. This is because German shepherd dogs are smart and easy to train. Dogs that work as police dogs, as guide dogs, or as search and rescue dogs need special training to learn these skills.

The German Shepherd Dog Today

German shepherd dogs had become popular around the world by the early twentieth century. During **World War I**, German shepherd dogs worked as guard dogs in the military.

German shepherd dogs became so popular because they could be trained for many different uses. They continue to help the military and the police in many countries. German shepherd dogs have a good sense of smell, which makes them valuable on search and rescue teams and for helping police find criminals and drugs. They also do well in contests that measure different abilities, such as tracking, herding, and obedience.

People often think German shepherd dogs are tough dogs because of their police work. However, they can be very gentle as pets and in their work as guide dogs for blind and deaf people. This breed has a long history of helping and working with people.

A Tough Breed?

Some people are afraid of German shepherd dogs and think they are **aggressive** dogs because they have played tough guard dogs in movies. One reason they have appeared in so many movies is because they can be easily trained, which makes them great actors. There are many examples of German shepherd dogs who have played heroes in movies. For example, a movie called *K-9* showed a German shepherd dog on the police force.

It is important to remember that no breed is mean by nature. However, some irresponsible owners do not know how to handle their German shepherd dogs. If German shepherd dogs are not trained properly or do not get enough exercise, they can misbehave or even become aggressive. Owners must be responsible and provide their German shepherd dogs with proper training and care.

German shepherd dogs are not naturally aggressive. Like all dogs, with proper training and care they can make wonderful family pets. Right: No matter which breed, any dog that has been mistreated or trained to attack can be a danger.

15

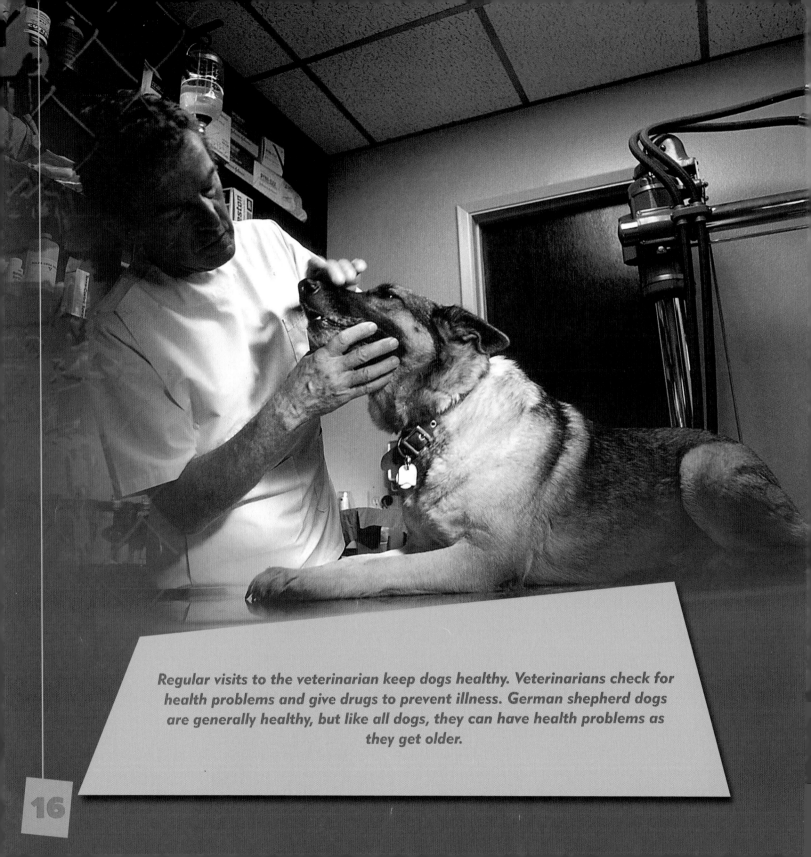

Regular visits to the veterinarian keep dogs healthy. Veterinarians check for health problems and give drugs to prevent illness. German shepherd dogs are generally healthy, but like all dogs, they can have health problems as they get older.

Caring for a German Shepherd Dog

Giving a dog good care is important no matter which breed it is. Good care includes providing shelter, water, healthy food, and lots of love. German shepherd dogs have thick coats that shed, so owners must **groom** them by brushing their coats at least once a week.

Owners must also make sure their dogs stay healthy by taking them to the **veterinarian** for regular checkups. German shepherd dogs have lots of energy and also must get plenty of exercise each day. If German shepherd dogs do not get enough exercise, they may act out by jumping, chewing, or barking. In addition to exercise, training is an important part of caring for a German shepherd dog.

DOG SAFETY TIPS

- Never approach a dog you do not know.
- When meeting a dog, offer the back of your hand for the dog to sniff.
- Speak softly, not loudly. Move gently, not suddenly.
- Never try to pet a dog through a fence.
- Never bother a dog while it is sleeping, eating, or sick.
- Do not pull at a dog's fur, ears, or tail. Never tease or hit a dog.
- Never approach a dog that is growling or showing its teeth. Back away slowly. Yelling and running can cause the dog to chase you or act aggressively.

Training a German Shepherd Dog

No matter what breed, all dogs need to be trained as puppies to follow certain commands, such as *sit*, *stay*, *heel*, *down*, and *come*. These basic commands help owners keep dogs well behaved and under control. German shepherd dogs that are household pets only need this basic training. German shepherd dogs that work in jobs, including guarding, police work, guiding, or pet therapy, need to have advanced training.

Another important part of raising a healthy German shepherd dog is **socialization**. Socialization means carefully bringing German shepherd puppies into contact with different people and dogs. Showing dogs many different sights, sounds, and smells helps them learn the difference between friendly and unfriendly people or situations. Socialization will also help prevent dogs from acting aggressively out of fear.

Socialization helps a German shepherd behave well around new people, animals, and settings. They will not act aggressively our of fear. They can safely play with new dogs, no matter the size.

This German shepherd dog is a search and rescue worker. It is helping to find people in fallen buildings after an earthquake in Mexico City. A search and rescue dog's excellent sense of smell and willingness to work can help it save many lives.

Heroic German Shepherd Dogs

German shepherd dogs have done many brave and **heroic** deeds. A great example of these heroic dogs is a K-9 police unit in Los Angeles. In 1994, there was an **earthquake**. Six German shepherd dogs that were part of the Metropolitan K-9 Platoon helped search an apartment building that had fallen down. The dogs found people trapped there and helped save them.

In Ohio a German shepherd dog was found wandering in the yard of Dorothy and Ray Ellis. The Ellises took the dog, whom they named Girl, into their home as a pet. One day Girl was outside with Ray. Girl came to the door of the house and began crying out for Dorothy. Girl led Dorothy outside, and Dorothy saw Ray had been hurt. Thanks to Girl, Dorothy was able to call for help in time. Girl helped save Ray's life.

Many famous people have owned German shepherd dogs, including President Franklin Delano Roosevelt and Sigmund Freud.

What a Dog!

There were more than 46,000 German shepherd dogs listed with the American Kennel Club in 2004. They are one of the top three breeds in the United States.

A great example of this breed is Zeus. When he was a puppy, Zeus was trained to be a police dog. He became a member of the New York Police Department's K-9 Unit. He also worked for the Federal Emergency Management Agency as a search and rescue dog. In addition to doing police work, Zeus was also a family pet. His owners thought Zeus was a great companion.

German shepherd dogs are a wonderful breed of dog that has a long history of helping people. From their work with police, to their work as guide dogs for the blind, German shepherd dogs have become valued working animals. They are caring and loving pets and are also winners in many contests. It is important to value and respect this smart and fearless breed.

Glossary

aggressive (uh-GREH-siv) Ready to fight.

ancestors (AN-ses-terz) Relatives who lived long ago.

bred (BRED) To have brought a male and a female animal together so they will have babies.

breed (BREED) A group of animals that look alike and have the same relatives.

domesticated (duh-MES-tuh-kayt-id) Raised to live with people.

earthquake (URTH-kwayk) A shaking of Earth's surface caused by the movement of large pieces of land called plates that run into each other.

groom (GROOM) To clean someone's body and make it neat and tidy.

heroic (hih-ROH-ik) Brave and noble.

K-9 (KAY-nyn) The name given to the groups of dogs that work with police.

muzzles (MUH-zuhlz) The part of animals' heads that come forward and include the nose.

pet therapy (PEHT THEHR-uh-pee) When people use animals to help them deal with certain problems.

socialization (soh-shuh-luh-ZAY-shun) Learning to be friendly.

veterinarian (veh-tuh-ruh-NER-ee-un) A doctor who treats animals.

World War I (WURLD WOR WUN) The war fought between the Allies and the Central Powers from 1914 to 1918.

Index

Web Sites

Due to the changing nature of Internet links, PowerKids Press has developed an online list of Web sites related to the subject of this book. This site is updated regularly. Please use this link to access the list: www.powerkidslinks.com/tdog/gshepherds/